O Canada!
Our home and native land!
True patriot love in all thy sons command.

With glowing hearts we see thee rise,
The True North strong and free!

From far and wide,
O Canada, we stand on guard for thee.

God keep our land glorious and free!
O Canada, we stand on guard for thee.

O Canada, we stand on guard for thee.

Oh, Canada!

Per-Henrik Gürth

Kids Can Press

Hello! Bonjour!

We live in Canada.

Our country's name comes from the Wendat–Haudenosaunee word for "village": *kanata*.

Canada's birthday is July 1, 1867

Did you know that Canada has two official languages? Yes! Oui! English and French.

Red and white are Canada's official colours.

This is Canada's flag. See? It's red and white.

Did you notice the maple leaf on the flag?
The maple leaf and the maple tree
are two symbols of Canada.

Each province and territory has
its own flag and symbols, too.

Canada is made up of
10 provinces and
3 territories.

Want to learn more? Let's take
a cross-Canada tour to explore!

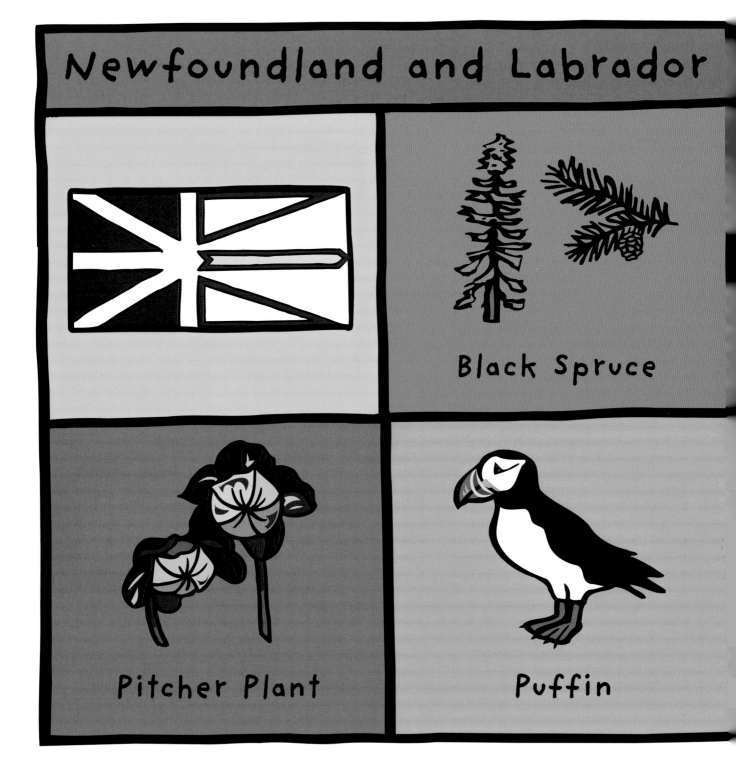

Newfoundland and Labrador

Black Spruce

Pitcher Plant

Puffin

Wave to whales at play
in Trinity Bay.

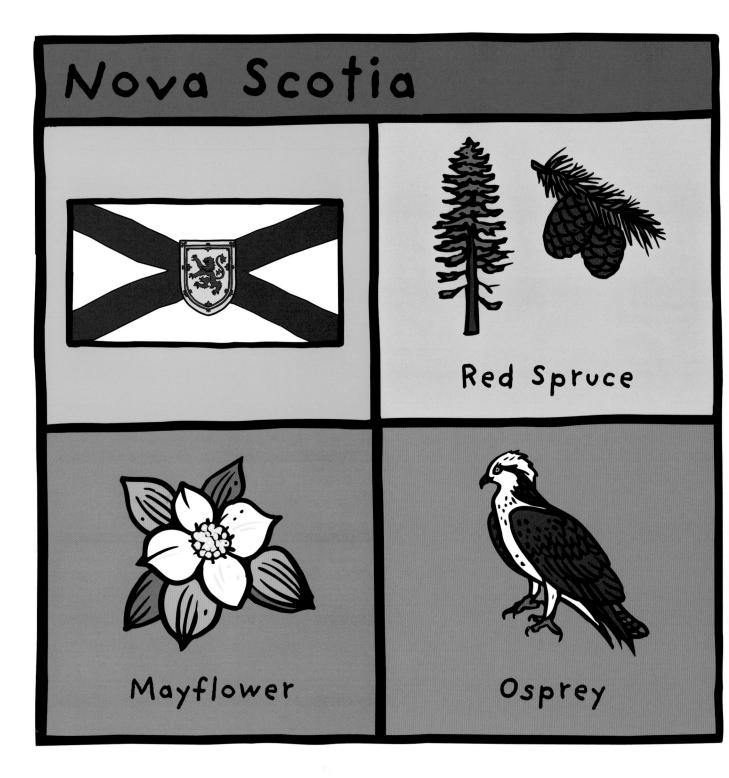

Nova Scotia

Red Spruce

Mayflower

Osprey

Prince Edward Island

Red Oak

Lady's-slipper

Blue Jay

Bike along red dirt roads on the South Shore.

New Brunswick

Balsam Fir

Purple Violet

Black-capped
Chickadee

Explore the sea floor at Hopewell Rocks. Neat!

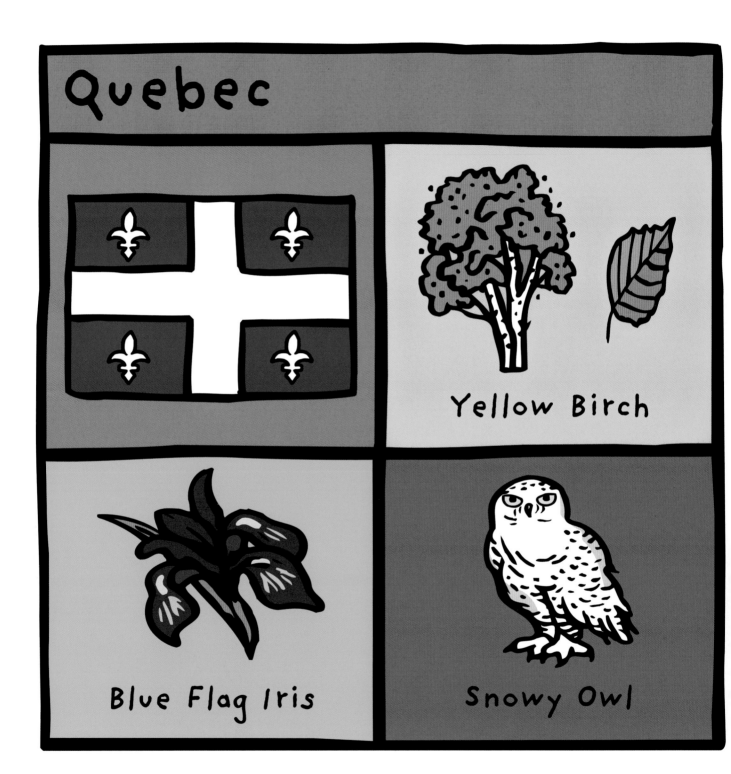

Quebec

Yellow Birch

Blue Flag Iris

Snowy Owl

Set sail in Quebec City.

Ontario

Eastern White Pine

White Trillium

Common Loon

Manitoba

White Spruce

Prairie Crocus

Great Gray Owl

Saskatchewan

White Birch

Western Red Lily

Sharp-tailed Grouse

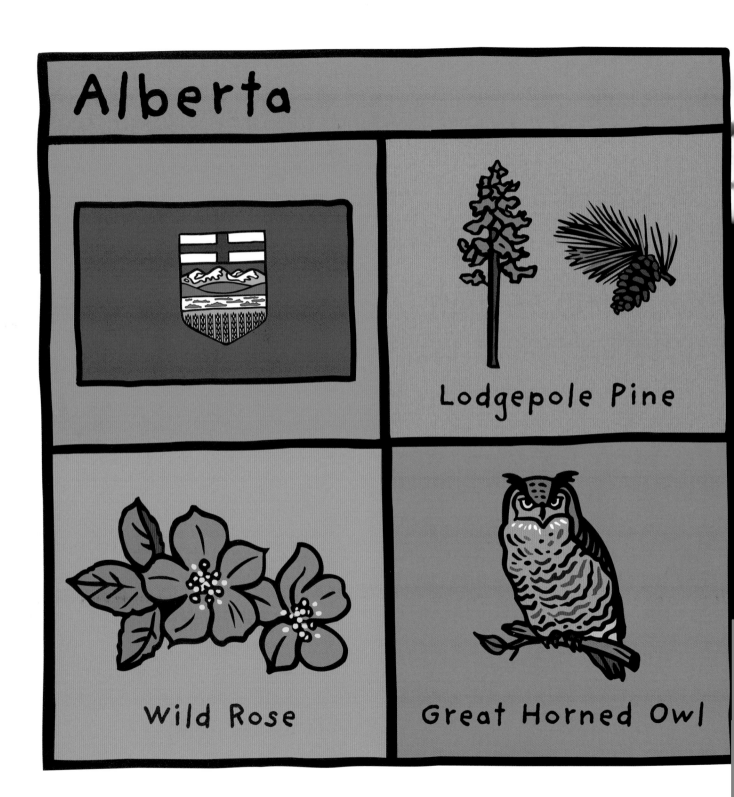

Alberta

Lodgepole Pine

Wild Rose

Great Horned Owl

Hunt for fossils
in Dinosaur Provincial Park.

British Columbia

Western Red Cedar

Pacific Dogwood

Steller's Jay

Hit the snowy slopes in Whistler. Woohoo!

Sub-alpine Fir

Fireweed

Common Raven

Northwest Territories

Tamarack

Mountain Avens

Gyrfalcon

Fly high over the taiga plains near Great Slave Lake.

Nunavut

Purple Saxifrage

Rock Ptarmigan

Oh, Canada!

NEWFOUNDLAND
AND LABRADOR

QUEBEC

PRINCE EDWARD ISLAND

NOVA SCOTIA

ARIO

NEW BRUNSWICK

Text © 2009 Kids Can Press
Illustrations © 2009 Per-Henrik Gürth

Kids Can Press acknowledges the financial support of the Government of Ontario, through the Ontario Media Development Corporation's Ontario Book Initiative; the Ontario Arts Council; the Canada Council for the Arts; and the Government of Canada, through the BPIDP, for our publishing activity.

Published in Canada by
Kids Can Press Ltd.
29 Birch Avenue
Toronto, ON M4V 1E2

Published in the U.S. by
Kids Can Press Ltd.
2250 Military Road
Tonawanda, NY 14150

www.kidscanpress.com

The artwork in this book was created in Adobe Illustrator.
The text is set in Providence-Sans Bold.

Written and edited by Yvette Ghione
Designed by Julia Naimska and Rachel Di Salle
Printed and bound in China

This book is smyth sewn casebound.

CM 09 0 9 8 7 6 5 4 3 2

Library and Archives Canada Cataloguing in Publication

Gürth, Per-Henrik
     Oh, Canada! / illustrated by Per-Henrik Gürth ;
written by Yvette Ghione.

Interest age level: For ages 3–7.
ISBN 978-1-55453-374-9

1. Canada—Juvenile literature. I. Ghione, Yvette II. Title.

FC58.G44 2009   j971   C2008-903324-8

Kids Can Press is a **Corus**™ Entertainment company

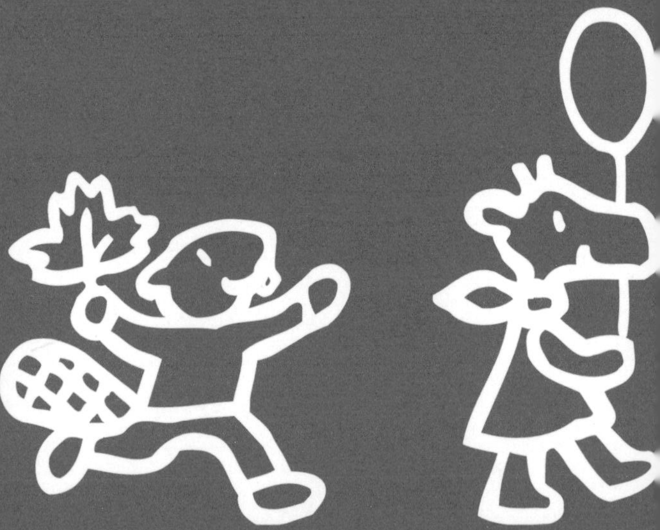